# Joseph
## the Dreamer

This book belongs to:

_____

**HARVEST HOUSE PUBLISHERS**
EUGENE, OREGON

Joseph and his family lived in Canaan. His father was called Jacob, and he had ten brothers at that time. Joseph was the youngest son, and so Jacob spent a lot of time with him.

**Joseph's coat was made of many different colors. What's your favorite color?**

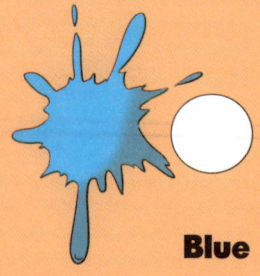

**Blue**

**Pink**

**Green**

One day Jacob had a very special robe made for Joseph. It was a beautiful coat made of every color you could possibly imagine.

When Joseph's brothers saw the beautiful coat, they became very jealous. They were so jealous that they became very cruel to Joseph and were never nice to him.

**Yellow**  **Red**  **Purple**

One night, Joseph had a strange dream. He dreamed that he and his brothers were working in the field, and suddenly their eleven sheaves of grain all bowed down to his sheaf of grain. Joseph told his brothers about the dream.

Joseph had another dream, and again he told his brothers about his dream. He told them that the sun, the moon, and the eleven stars all bowed down to him.

**What things did Joseph see in his dreams?**

**Sheaf of grain.**

**Star**

A couple of days later, Jacob asked Joseph to go and check on his brothers in the field. When the brothers saw him coming, they came up with a plan to kill him.
Joseph's oldest brother did not want them to kill him, so they came up with another plan to throw him down a well.

**Joseph was sold and taken to Egypt as a slave. Can you see what he passed on the way?**

When Joseph caught up to them, they tore off his coat and threw him into the well.

A while later some people came who wanted things to sell in Egypt. The brothers decided to sell Joseph to these people. They ripped his coat and covered it with animal blood. Then they told their father an animal had killed him.

Joseph was sold to Potiphar, an assistant to the Pharaoh of Egypt. He began as Potiphar's slave, but with God's help, he was soon put in charge of all that Potiphar owned.

Potiphar's wife was jealous and made up lies about Joseph. Potiphar believed his wife and had Joseph thrown into prison.

**The butler dreamed that there were three branches. All of a sudden, the leaves grew, then blossoms, then grapes. When the grapes ripened, he squeezed them into the Pharaoh's cup.**

**Grapes**

While Joseph was in prison, a butler and a baker were also put in the same cell. Both the butler and the baker had strange dreams. They told Joseph about their dreams, and with God's help, he explained what the dreams meant.

Goblet

**The baker dreamed that he was carrying three baskets. In the top basket there were lots of tasty buns, but the birds kept eating them.**

Baker

Joseph remained in jail for a long time, until one night the Pharaoh himself had strange dreams. He asked if there was anyone wise enough to tell him what his dreams meant. Joseph was brought before him.

Joseph listened to the Pharaoh's dreams, and then with God's help, he explained what they meant. He told the Pharaoh there would be seven years of plentiful food, and this would be followed by seven years of famine.

**The Pharaoh had two strange dreams.**

**In one he dreamed there were seven strong sheaves of wheat followed by seven withered and burnt sheaves of wheat.**

The Pharaoh was pleased to understand and thought Joseph was a very wise man indeed. So he decided to put Joseph in charge of the whole of Egypt, and he dressed him in fine royal robes.

**In another he dreamed that there were seven fat cows followed by seven skinny cows.**

For the next seven years, there was good rainfall and the crops grew and grew. Joseph told the people to gather the overflowing food. In every city they gathered up the food and stored it in barns for the years of famine, which were to come.

**What kind of crops did they grow?**

**Wheat**

One day the rain stopped and the land became dry. The crops dried up and died, and there was a shortage of food. Fortunately, Egypt had lots of food in storage, thanks to Joseph. Joseph opened the barns and sold the stored food to those who needed it.

**Corn**

**Vines**

People came from all over to buy grain from Joseph. After some time, Joseph's brothers came before Joseph and asked for grain. They did not recognize their brother.

The brothers all bowed before Joseph, just as Joseph's dreams had shown they would. Joseph wanted to see if his brothers had become good people.

He asked them to leave their youngest brother with him as a slave. The brothers refused and said they would become his slaves themselves. Joseph was pleased they had become good, and so he told his brothers who he was.

They did not believe Joseph at first. They were afraid, but Joseph embraced them and asked them to fetch his father.

When Jacob arrived in Egypt and saw Joseph, he cried in relief and thanked God for the wonderful news.